AuthorHouse™
1663 Liberty Drive
Bloomington, IN 47403
www.authorhouse.com
Phone: 1 (800) 839-8640

Cover Illustration by Navi' Robins.

Published by AuthorHouse 09/20/2018

ISBN: 978-1-5462-5892-6 (sc)
978-1-5462-5891-9 (e)

Library of Congress Control Number: 2018910591

Print information available on the last page.

authorHOUSE®

I HAVE BIG DREAMS

Rianna Dreams of Competing in the Olympics

Rianna Facey & Tywanna Gardner

I have big dreams.

I dream of going to the Olympics one day and competing on a gymnastics team.

I practice gymnastics every day. I love to show my mom my cartwheels and splits.

I started taking gymnastics when I was 8 years old.

I'm 9 years old now.

I do my cartwheels indoors and outdoors.

Wherever I go I practice my gymnastics.

My coach says I do very well.

When I went to summer camp last year the teacher had the class try gymnastics.

The teachers told my mom that I was very good and that she should sign me up for gymnastics classes right away.

They told her that I was good enough to compete on a gymnastics team.

She signed me up and I took classes every week.

The coach said I was good too.

When I’m not doing gymnastics. I like to make slime.

I make all kinds of slime.

Some of it is gooey and others can be stretched out. I make all kinds of colors too.

I love to make slime. When I go to a friend's house they ask me to bring some of my slime.

I don’t mind sharing. I can always make some more.

After I make slime, I practice my gymnastics.

One day I hope to make it to the Olympics to compete on an Olympic team.

For now I'll just keep practicing.

I have big dreams.

What do you dream?

Printed in the United States
By Bookmasters